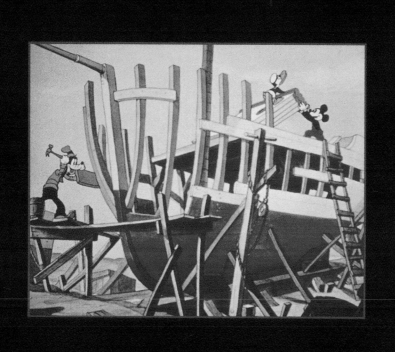

"To be on the deck of a great ship on a star-filled night in the middle of a great ocean is as close to magic as there ever is. I can't be certain whether Walt Disney envisaged such a prospect for the company he founded, but I'd like to believe he did."

—Michael D. Eisner
Chairman and CEO, The Walt Disney Company

DISNEY MAGIC

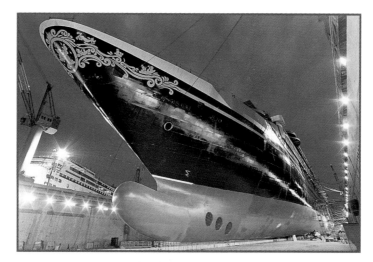

THE LAUNCHING OF A DREAM

by John Heminway

A WELCOME BOOK

HYPERION

NEW YORK

For information address:
Hyperion, 114 Fifth Avenue, New York, NY 10011

Produced by Welcome Enterprises, Inc.
588 Broadway, New York, NY 10012

Project Directors: Sara Baysinger,
Hiro Clark Wakabayashi
Designer: Mary Tiegreen
Hyperion Editor: Wendy Lefkon
Hyperion Assistant Editor: Robin Friedman

Cover and pages 6–7: Rendering of the *Disney Magic*
by Stephen J. Card.
Page 1: Film still from Walt Disney's *Boat Builders*, 1938.
Page 3: The *Disney Magic* under construction in Marghera, Italy.

Pages 8–9, 22, 36 courtesy Corbis-Bettmann; pages 58–59, 61,
66–67, 70–73, 79–80, 88–89 courtesy Zindman and Fremont; page
63 (left, top to bottom) courtesy Shaun Chappell; page 63 (right)
courtesy Joseph Kugielsky; pages 68–69 courtesy Laumont Labs.

Printed in Singapore by Tien Wah Press
2 4 6 8 10 9 7 5 3 1

Contents

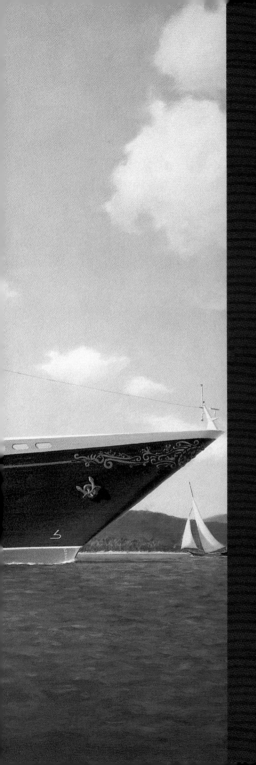

PREFACE

G reat ships should make the heart race. Ships are the largest things on earth that move—move not just their own bulk, but people, cargoes and, with luck, the human spirit.

The *Disney Magic* is a ship that was prepared in the kitchen of imagination with remarkable ingredients: a dash of hardheadedness enriched by scoop after scoop of whimsy, nostalgia, innovation, fun and, yes, magic. From the start, the *Disney Magic* has been dedicated to launching the imaginative spirit.

Virtually all who brought this astonishing ship to creation will admit to moments when they stopped dead in their corporate tracks, closed their eyes, threw common sense and convention to the wind, all to dream. From individual moments of inspiration, they each recalled childlike notions of great ships. With eyes shut, they had gone to sea—metaphorically, at least—onboard galleons, Liberty ships, royal yachts. When each emerged from such flights of fantasy, these captains of industry had discovered a way to add their personal inspiration to a ship that, ultimately, would be like no other.

Eventually, all dreams became one: the *Disney Magic* would claim parentage to the era of great ocean liners, but would set new standards in the world of cruising, far into the 21st century.

While the grandeur of the past would give a language to the ship, a cadence to its design and a setting for its story, it would be most distinguished by the pixie-dust magic of Disney. Through each space on the ship, the past, present and future would be glorified in ways never

Above: THE S.S. *IMPERATOR.*
Left: THE S.S. *NORMANDIE,*
THE MOST ELEGANT SHIP OF
THE 1930S, IN NEW YORK.
Below: THE S.S. *CARINTHIA*
IN NEW YORK HARBOR.

before attempted. Its inventors were charged to create "wows" by turning history into fantasy.

And what a history it was! For more than a century ocean liners were the fundamental link between Europe and America. Tales of generations that made the Atlantic crossing to the New World aboard ships such as the *Imperator, Mauretania, Lucania, Carinthia* and the *Berengaria* abound. These sea passages promised glamour, discovery, rebirth on a grand scale and still serve as the defining moments of entire families—the pivotal journey at the onset of the American experience.

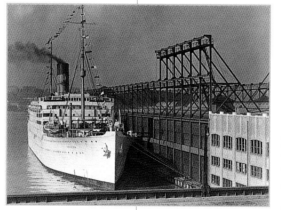

For those not fortunate enough to have shipped aboard a great ocean liner, the magnificent Atlantic crossings of the past were transferred to our collective experience, thanks to movies. The drama, comedy and romance of *An Affair To Remember, Dodsworth, Shall We Dance,* and *Monkey Business* were set onboard these great transatlantic stages. When Cary Grant and Deborah Kerr meet we know theirs will be a great love story. Mere pranks by the Marx Brothers are elevated to high jinks onboard their ship of fools. When Ginger and Fred dance, they dance free of time and geography, halfway to the stars.

So it will be with the *Disney Magic.* Its creators

Above: BUILT IN 1907, THE S.S. *MAURETANIA* WAS AT THAT
TIME THE LARGEST PASSENGER SHIP IN THE WORLD.

have envisaged a magnificent seagoing stage set. The tradition of extraordinary family entertainment set forth by Disney's master storytellers—from beloved animated features to theme parks—finds a brand new home aboard the *Disney Magic*. Be it the spacious, family-friendly staterooms, the innovative shipboard dining program, or the unique children's areas and activities, the Disney touch can be felt everywhere.

Paying homage to the legendary transatlantic ocean liner, the *Disney Magic* has transformed the hallmarks of classicism into preconditions for the future. The sleekness that was once essential for liners in pursuit of the coveted Blue Riband speed award is now exalted as modern nautical grace—the bow sleek and arching, decks sweeping, the stern as if in flight. At last, a ship's bridge will resume its rightful place as powerhouse, nerve center, genius. Portholes will be restored as portholes, this time playfully large, and funnels—count them, two—restored to yesterday's grandeur, but redesigned as emblems of the future, in a timeless style that is quintessentially Disney.

The *Disney Magic* is a story all her own. In these pages you will discover the remarkable tale of how she came to be, the imagination that inspired her and the great enterprise of will and whimsy that makes her already a celebrated blend of nostalgia and innovation.

❖ *DISNEY MAGIC* ❖
MARGHERA, ITALY, SPRING 1997.

CHAPTER ONE

BIRTH OF THE DREAM

1

On a humid day in late spring of 1997, Wing T. Chao, Walt Disney Imagineering's Executive Vice President of Master Planning, Architecture and Design, took a small speedboat from his hotel in Venice, Italy, across a lagoon to the industrial port of Marghera. For the last four years he and so many others at The Walt Disney Company had lived with a dream—of building a great ship that would be the first of many to set new standards in the world of cruise vacations. If anyone knew the ship's design, space by space, deck by deck, bow to stern, it was Chao.

Yet he was unable to restrain his excitement. When his boat rounded the headland and the yet-to-be-inaugurated *Disney Magic* came into view, he could feel the breath escaping his lungs while he uttered, "Wow."

When asked who deserves credit for the birth of the *Disney Magic*, Chao is likely to quote from half a Chinese proverb: "Success has 100 parents."

When pressed, Chao is modest about his own contribution, but insistent that others—among them Larry Murphy—deserve the initial credit for steering The Walt Disney Company into the cruise business.

As Executive Vice President and Chief Strategic Officer of The Walt Disney Company, Lawrence P. Murphy's role is to guide Disney's expansion into new business arenas. Murphy is a driven executive known to be relentless in his pursuit of perfection. He constantly challenges those around him to greater ends.

Larry Murphy was well aware of the American public's infatuation with cruising—large, white ships, exotic ports of call, opalescent seas, sumptuous meals, Las Vegas-style shows. Murphy had first watched the industry grow during the early '80s while with the Marriott Corporation. When he began at Disney in 1985, he vowed to explore the business more thoroughly. At first, the timing was less than perfect: The Walt Disney Company was then embarking on many other business initiatives to diversify beyond the theme park business, which then represented nearly 75 percent of its earnings. The company's attention was elsewhere.

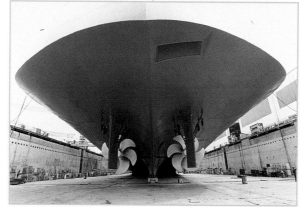

Above: VIEW OF THE SHIP'S HULL SHOWING THE PROPELLERS IN POSITION.
Opposite: BOW VIEW OF THE *DISNEY MAGIC.*

Disney had already dabbled in the cruise business. For a number of years it had participated in a licensing arrangement with a cruise line whose three vintage ships were based in Port Canaveral, an hour's drive from Walt Disney World. Disney characters had been featured aboard these vessels; Mickey, Minnie, Donald and Goofy appeared in the line's promotional material. For better or worse, the public dubbed these vessels "Disney ships."

Disney executives were concerned that under a licensing arrangement they would not be able to completely control and assure the quality of the onboard experience. "In the end," recalls Michael Eisner, "I said to my colleagues, 'Let's pull out.'"

With the termination of the licensing agreement, Larry Murphy, Al Weiss, President of Walt Disney World Resort, and Frank Ioppolo, Executive Vice President Legal and General Counsel, Walt Disney Attractions, initiated a full-scale exploration of a more substantial partnership with two large cruise lines. The negotiations with these giants persisted from January until November 1992.

Michael Eisner joined in the research. It was clear to him the cruise industry would make a strategic fit with Walt Disney World, situated a convenient ride from several deepwater ports. The opportunities were many: cruise enthusiasts might visit Walt Disney World for the first time; regular Walt Disney World visitors might extend their stays, adding a cruise to their trip; a one-week package combining a Walt Disney World vacation with a cruise could become the ultimate family holiday.

To a large extent, Michael Eisner's attention was focused on the "look" of existing cruise ships. Known for architectural acuity and design boldness, Eisner studied every cruise ship he could spot in Nassau and Miami. "They didn't look like ships to me," he recalls. "Hotels, yes. All glass, and see-through elevators . . . These ships were more about Vegas than about the sea.

I know they are hugely popular and I could see why people loved going on them, but it simply wasn't for me. Every fiber in my body revolted against building such a ship.

"There was another concern I had at the time about forming a partnership with an existing cruise line. We at Disney overspend on 'guest experience.' We deliver to our guests more than they expect. I didn't believe a partner—any partner—would understand. They would consider our spending over the top."

"A cruise line is a natural extension of our business," insists Judson Green, the President of Walt Disney Attractions. Recognized for a sharp analytical mind, a clear binocular view of the company's future, this former C.P.A. had been eyeing a Disney-owned cruise business as a logical expansion of the resort business. In 1993 "we woke up and realized we knew how to cruise from a functional point of view—in respect to hotel, food and beverage, merchandise, entertainment and worldwide sales. If you think about all the disciplines reflected onboard a ship, we had them all except for one—an ability to 'drive the ship'—and that we could acquire. Our core competency is guest satisfaction—it's something we realized could easily be transferred to the high seas."

"I can remember the turning point," recalls Wing Chao. "It was at a meeting in Glendale, [California] in November 1992." Many of Disney's top executives, Frank Wells, Michael Eisner, Al Weiss and Frank Ioppolo were there. The group had three options from which to choose—a Disney partnership with a distinguished cruise line; a resolution by Disney to form a cruise line of its own; or a decision that The Walt Disney Company should steer clear of the cruise line business altogether.

Larry Murphy's intensity was palpable. He was single-minded. "I made the presentation," he remembers. "By now, after all I'd learned, there was no doubt which way I leaned . . . I believed we should create our own cruise line." Michael Eisner responded to the presentation with several questions, and then, with Frank Wells's consent, made the decision, "Let's do it ourselves."

"It was a courageous move," says Murphy. "We had no direct experience in the cruise business and with Michael's 'OK,' our financial commitment was now one billion dollars!"

Disney Cruise Line became reality.

❖ Magical Visions ❖

Ship design concept created by Hartmut Esslinger of frogdesign. This design helped establish the signature elements of the *Disney Magic*, including the exaggerated bridge, classic funnels and elongated bowline.

CHAPTER TWO

CHOICES

2

I n view of what was to come, November's billion-dollar nod might have been the easiest decision of all. The look of the predestined cruise ship (or ships), where these would be based, their destinations and, most important, how a nautical business would dovetail seamlessly into the entertainment world of Disney were yet to be defined.

Success would depend largely on the team assembled by Larry Murphy and Al Weiss. With Wing Chao's advice, they hired architect Mike Reininger as Vice President, Product Development, giving him the responsiblility for the ship's design.

This was still a team of innocents. Chao admitted that his familiarity with cruising came

from two cruise vacations of his own and from watching "Love Boat" on television.

Reininger had previously dedicated himself to the distinctive architectural vision of The Walt Disney Company, working with noted architects such as Michael Graves and Robert Stern. As for his knowledge of the cruise industry, he would wanly admit that his only experience had been a Caribbean cruise he and his wife had won as a door prize. "And I can assure you it was not a memorable experience."

"I became known as the man of 10,000 questions," recalls Reininger. He hired ship brokers Jean-Bernard Raoust and Jean-Francois Cristeau of the Paris-based firm Barry Rogliano Salles to introduce him to leading naval architects and to

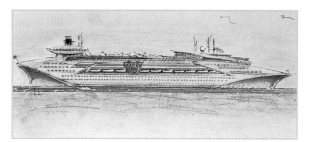

Above: CONCEPT DESIGN BY NJAL EIDE AFTER THE CHOICE HAD BEEN MADE TO PURSUE CREATING A TRADITIONAL SHIP.

Left: FOLLOWING EIDE'S CONCEPT DESIGN, DISNEY CRUISE LINE COMMISSIONED THIS OIL RENDERING TO CREATE A REALISTIC VERSION OF EIDE'S WORK.

Above right: THE DRAMATIC LINES IN THIS CONCEPT SKETCH BY PETER YRAN AND BJORN STORBRAATEN REFLECT A VERY FUTURISTIC VISION THAT THE TEAM WOULD ULTIMATELY REJECT IN FAVOR OF A MORE CLASSICAL APPROACH.

arrange shipyard tours around the world. "It dawned on me soon after I began that our mission was not a construction process but much bigger—industrial, in fact. This was not about building a building. The scale, the impact on a workforce, the effect on an economy—it was enormous. So too our task. My site visits also gave me my first inkling of how Disney might have an original impact on design . . ."

While Reininger was accumulating a formidable number of frequent-flyer miles in pursuit of a shipbuilding education, Al Weiss and Larry Murphy were marshaling the management team. Early in 1994, they interviewed a number of cruise executives. One was Art Rodney, former President of Princess Cruise Lines, later CEO of Crystal Cruise Line, the industry's biggest recent start-up. The seasoned Rodney, one of the spiritual parents of the "Love Boat" phenomenon, met with Al Weiss and Larry Murphy for breakfast at a hotel in Los Angeles. Weiss recalls, "We had been trying to find someone who had a wealth of experience, who understood quality and had undergone the process of business start-up as well as new ship construction. All these requirements were vital, and Art filled all the bills."

In mid-May 1994, Reininger was joined by Jon Rusten, recently of the Norwegian Cruise Line. Rusten had more than 20 years of experience in the field of ship design and construction and understood the

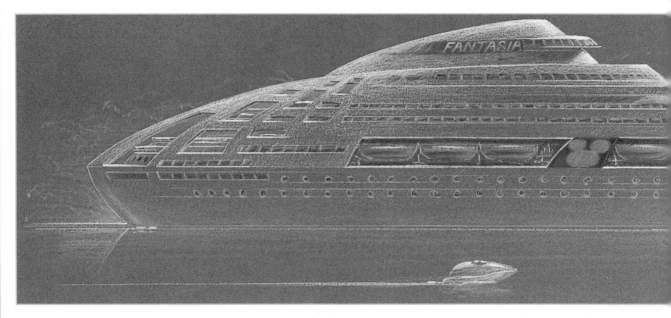

Above and below:
FANCIFUL DESIGN CON-
CEPTS BY WALT DISNEY
IMAGINEERS. THE S.S.
FANTASIA (*above*) WAS
THE CLEAR WINNER IN
MARKET RESEARCH
POLLS.

delicate balance between the look and heft of a hull and the spaces that would occupy it.

The team had narrowed the architectural field to three companies, all Scandinavian. The distinguished naval architects were challenged to a design competition. Njal Eide from Oslo, Norway, the partnership of Peter Yran and Bjorn Storbraaten, also from Oslo, and Robert Tillberg of Viken, Sweden, were invited to Orlando to tour Walt Disney World properties—hotels, restaurants and attractions—to demonstrate Disney craftsmanship, dedication to theme, whimsy and attention to detail.

Fantasy ruled the day. Having looked at many different cruise ships in production, Reininger's personal conclusion was that most suffered from self-imposed industrial constraints, that they all appeared to

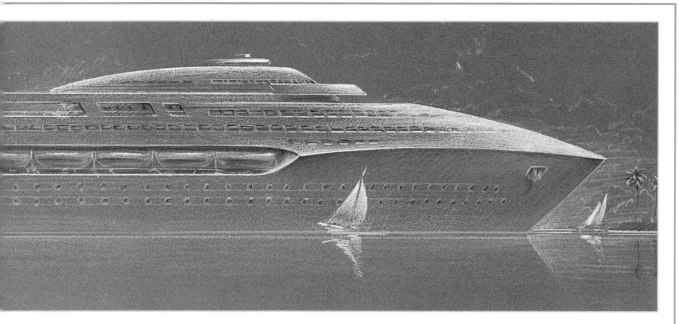

be built around a framework that was, at best, utilitarian. There seemed little romance, "little sense of Hollywood in contemporary cruise ship design." Yes, they were stylistically fleet, even elegant at times, but structurally they had been driven by a simple formula of compressing the maximum number of cabins into a hull. Where was the fantasy? "All we had to do to make a statement," concluded Reininger, "was to go 180 degrees from the common direction of the industry."

The three architectural finalists were challenged to let their imaginations run free; the results of the first round of this competition are simply breathtaking. Imagine a ship inspired by

Below: NAVAL ARCHITECT ROBERT TILLBERG TOOK A WHIMSICAL APPROACH TO A CLASSIC SHIP, USING TRADITIONAL COLOR WITH PLAYFUL LINES IN HIS DESIGN.

Above and top: CONCEPT DESIGNS BY ROBERT TILLBERG, GENERATED AFTER DISNEY CRUISE LINE HAD SETTLED ON BUILDING A CLASSIC SHIP. THE TOP DESIGN SHOWS THE COLOR AND SIGNATURE ELEMENTS OF THE SHIP'S TWO FUNNELS AND SLEEK BOW.

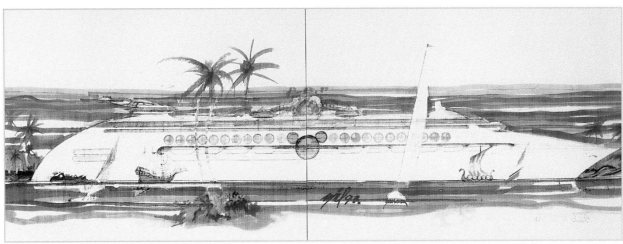

Captain Nemo's submarine in *20,000 Leagues Under the Sea*, another that would suggest a citrus plantation grown in an aquarium, another that purports to transform the ship's funnel into the Magic Kingdom, yet another that conjures up a sinister spaceship fed on a diet of steroids.

Above: EARLY CONCEPT DESIGN BY NJAL EIDE.

❖ ROYAL CALLINGS ❖

THE STATELY LINES AND INTERIORS OF THE *QUEEN MARY* SET THE STANDARD
FOR ANY OCEAN LINER THAT WOULD CALL ITSELF CLASSIC.

CHAPTER THREE

BIRTH OF THE MODERN CLASSIC

The three architects flew to Los Angeles and presented their selections directly to Michael Eisner. He shuffled through the pack of images and rejected them all. Njal Eide remembers his words: "Go home and make a modern classic." Others recall his summary exhortation: "I want you to out-tradition tradition."

Indeed, "out-tradition tradition" became a rallying cry for Disney Cruise Line.

Michael Eisner recalls his thought process at the time. "I know exactly what I was thinking about. I wanted our ship to bring back a feeling of the great times. I can remember seeing my grandparents off on the *Queen Mary* to Europe. I went down to the dock and I can recall the bustle, vast steamer trunks carried aboard. "Later, I was on the last voyage of the *Mauretania*. It was enormous fun. That image of the classic ship and the great ocean passage has stayed with me. It is the romance I feel people are seeking."

This romance was what was foremost to Eisner. It was not exactly what the architects had expected. Now, somewhat stunned by his rejection, they returned to Scandinavia for another attempt.

"It was totally unusual for me to work with three architects simultaneously," recalls Jon Rusten, the Disney Cruise Line's Director, Development and New Buildings. "They, too, had never worked this way before. Most architects work alone after the owner gives them a set of load requirements. The architect's task is then to build a framework around that space . . . We came at this project differently—we had to create a look and then we would make the spaces and the hull work to our needs. That is what has made this job a very inspiring experience for me."

At first glance, the architect least likely to succeed under the Michael Eisner directive was Njal Eide. "My specialty is the modern ship. The way I had interpreted Disney was very futuristic—everything on the top decks movable and the ship profile resembling a graceful

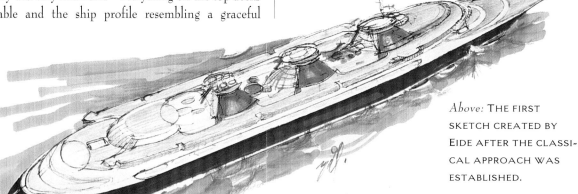

I do futuristic.' Then he came back with a winner."

"In many ways, I think Wing was the inspirer of the team," Eide says. "What the others didn't know is that as a young boy, I had spent a lot of time looking at and drawing traditional ships. The basic black hull with the white superstructure and red trim was very familiar to me.

Above: THE FIRST SKETCH CREATED BY EIDE AFTER THE CLASSICAL APPROACH WAS ESTABLISHED.

swan. No one believed I would be able to make the transition to what Michael Eisner wanted . . ."

Wing Chao remembers pressing for a second round of drawings. "Personally, I thought Eide was a visionary. I felt if I pushed him, he would come around to the Disney goal. He kept saying, 'I don't do nostalgic ships.

"So, returning home on the plane, I made a sketch. Fourteen days later, the design team came over to my studio and saw my finished drawings. 'Could you make a model?' they asked. I did, and my son flew to Orlando as its courier."

All three architects were represented in Orlando as detailed models were presented to the then fledgling Disney Cruise Line team in a makeshift boardroom.

"At the time, I was not a champion of the classic design," remembers Art Rodney. "I was in favor of a Nordic, futuristic, look. I didn't think the classic design was appropriate."

But Rodney was surprised. What Njal Eide had

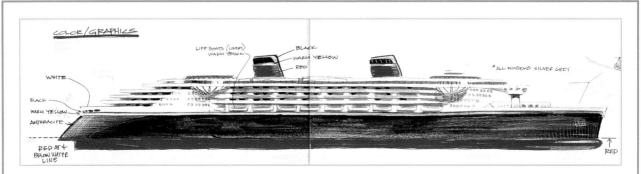

Above, right and below: THESE SHIP DESIGN BOARDS WERE CREATED BY FROGDESIGN FOR THEIR PRESENTATION TO DISNEY CRUISE LINE. THEY HELPED TO ESTABLISH A GUIDE FOR THE OVERALL COLOR SCHEME AND THE SHAPE OF THE FUNNELS, BRIDGE AND BOW.

achieved seemed impossible. His model possessed the hallmarks of the great traditional ships of the past but it exuded a contemporary feel.

Bjorn Storbraaten, his competitor, saw the Eide model and understood completely why it worked: "Njal was able to absorb the core of Disney. I thought it was wonderful . . ."

Even Robert Tillberg, whose model rested along-side Eide's, was able to spot the winner. "I thought Njal had done a great job. I was envious of him . . ."

Above: MODEL OF TOP DECKS BY YRAN AND STORBRAATEN.

Opposite: STUDY MODEL BY MARITIME REPLICAS.

These pages: VERY
ACCURATE IN THEIR
DETAIL, THESE SHIP
MODELS WERE CREATED
TO 1/200TH SCALE BY
MARITIME REPLICAS.

Njal Eide had included two signature funnels on his ship. From the start, they became a focal point. On modern vessels, only one funnel is necessary; in most cases these solitary funnels are disguised so completely they all but disappear. While Eide had made his two funnels graceful and sleek, they were, incontrovertibly, funnels. In fact, they begged the question among Disney Cruise Line executives: Should there be three? In the end, the two funnels were thought the right number—a statement of classicism, history, authenticity.

Njal Eide was asked to make a few slight modifications to his model; soon he had produced a second version. This modern classic exudes the future. It is streamlined, powerful with a raking bow and two funnels, swept back, and has a stern that had been inspired by a memory of the Norwegian American Line's S.S. *Stavangerfiord.* "This old-time cruiser was named after the region of southwestern Norway that's the place of my birth. As a result, I felt close to this ship; in my hands, it's long-ago stern could thus become modern."

"We had reduced the ship to key signatures," Mike Reininger remembers. In addition to the black hull and the two funnels, he was especially delighted with the positioning of key elements of the superstructure that allowed for a "sculpturing mass" in the area of the bridge, a geometry that fell away towards the ship's aft. This "stepped-up" design gave it a profile altogether modern.

Njal Eide looks at his model and says: "In the old days what made liners so special was the placement of lifeboats high up. It gives the ship a classic look. Now, for reasons related to safety the lifeboats must be located far below, on the promenade deck. So how could I create that classic look within the letter of law? I therefore chose to place huge bay windows on those

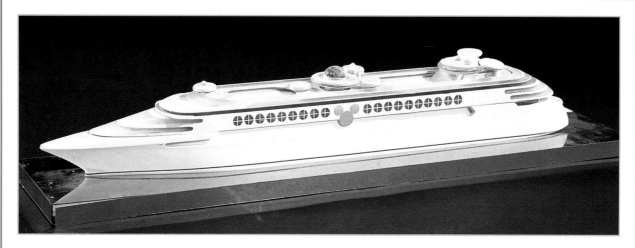

THIS WAS THE FIRST MODEL CRAFTED BY NJAL EIDE
TO EXPRESS HIS IDEA OF A SLEEK CLASSIC.

top decks and I divided those windows into modules, each about 12 meters long, cantilevered, each suggesting life boats."

In the end, the past is not described but suggested. Each element, whether funnel, porthole, lifeboat, bow, stern is interpreted for the future. Mike Reininger likes to describe the relationship in terms of automobiles. "Think of the new Ford Mustang or the Mazda Miata—classic cars reexpressed for the future. When someone looks at the Miata, one conjures the TR6, even though you know instantly that, unlike the TR6, this heir is thoroughly modern and possesses all essential contemporary features—air bags, disc brakes and so forth.

"So too with our ship. It expresses the glamour of the past, but even when you see it from a distance, you know it's not an old ship. It's a modern expression of the classic."

"But I thought we were only 85 percent of where we wanted to be," recalls Reininger. "Even though we had broken the designers out of their comfort zones, we kept running into naval architectural bias and preconception. It seemed to us we needed to turbocharge the process."

Dr. Hartmut Esslinger of frogdesign is sometimes known as industrial design's "bad boy." He enjoys reexamining the shapes of commonplace and beloved icons, then reinventing them. He is credited with the redesign, for instance, of Apple Computer's Macintosh, Rosenthal china, Sony's Trinitron televisions, Louis Vuitton luggage, dental chairs, Lotto machines, even toilets. He had never redesigned a ship.

"I looked at the winning model and, while I was impressed by it, I had a sense it needed more," Esslinger recalls after his first meeting in late 1994. "A cruise ship should be extrovert. It should allude to traditional vessels, but it should also look towards the future . . .

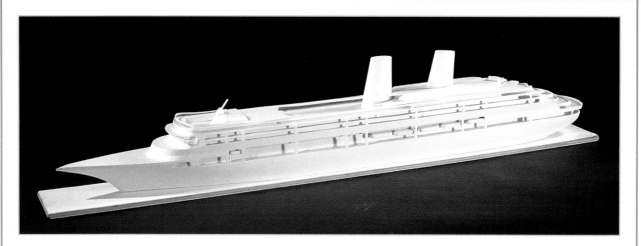

THIS EARLY MODEL BY ROBERT TILLBERG WAS GENERATED
BASED ON THE IDEA OF A CLASSIC VESSEL.

I call this thought process retro-futurism.

"An object this large—a ship—should be like a person you want to be with. It should have human qualities. The more an object responds to the body, the more we like it . . . The bridge, for one. People should know where to find the brain of the ship. That's a transparency people want. People also want to be in command. The bridge and the ship should hearken you to move on into a new world. Such a feel is badly missing on most cruise ships of today."

Esslinger took the existing bridge design and, in effect, blew it up, both in size and in look, much as the flight deck of the 747 has been enlarged beyond the requirements of aerodynamics, to suggest control, power, indeed, brain.

You would expect naval architect Njal Eide to have been outraged when he saw Esslinger's modification of his vision. On the contrary. "We have to credit frogdesign with the wheelhouse," reports Eide, with absolute conviction. "I thought their idea was good. The deckhouse became two-story and negative—negative in the sense it seems to slope in the wrong direction. It gives the deckhouse a strong, dramatic feel."

Bjorn Storbraaten also appreciated frogdesign's contribution to the bridge: "It creates a trademark. It sets the ship apart from everything that floats. It's not serious . . . it's playful."

Among Esslinger's other contributions was color. "I recognized the traditional colors of classic ship hulls were black. I think that, for the future, black is too sinister, too depressing, especially on a Disney ship. I selected a color that was 87 percent black, the rest blue." As a result, the ship will virtually change colors, depending on the time of day, weather and position. The variation of the color is astonishingly subtle: no one will doubt it is both classic and inventive.

The final model was illuminated by gold filigree on both bow and stern. Only one liner ever sported such decoration, and it was hardly a liner. The *Stella Polaris* was built by Norway's Bergen Line in 1927 to carry a mere 165 passengers, mostly on North Cape cruises. The filigree was even then a folly, a stylization to suggest a millionaire-class luxury yacht. Its application to the Disney ship demonstrates serendipity of design. The Disney ship is the synthesis of many nautical icons, adopted from various times and ships—some even imaginary; collectively, they suggest no one time or place, but a vessel for all—indeed, the ultimate ship. Robert Tillberg looked at the model and concluded: "Rarely do you meet a company with such a strong will to create the right profile. It took us so long to find the right track. The result was . . . a fantastic ship."

When the model was shown to Michael Eisner, the reaction was instant: "That's it." In a flash, Eisner had recognized the ship design that would wear the name "Disney."

With the exterior look established, it was time to

choose a shipbuilder. Simultaneously, attention was turned toward the ship's interior spaces. Traditionally, shipboard spaces are designed by one, maybe two, people—generally from a pool of naval architects, many of them Scandinavian, all acutely aware of shipboard limitations with respect to material and space. Either Tillberg, Yran and Storbraaten or Eide was the obvious choice. But this was a Disney ship—its very first—and a new approach, radically different from all others, was possible.

Above: THIS GRAPHIC RENDERING OF THE *DISNEY MAGIC* WAS USED BY DISNEY CRUISE LINE FOR ITS EARLY PRO-MOTIONAL LITERATURE.

❖ MAJESTIC VIEWS ❖

THE *DISNEY MAGIC* IN DRYDOCK.

CHAPTER FOUR

THE DREAM BECOMES STEEL

Many shipyards responsible for the renowned ocean liners of the past have themselves slipped into the limbo of history. Britain's Clydebank yards are today idle. Similarly, the United States has failed to stay competitive in the large civilian ship industry. In place of many bygone shipyards are others that have prevailed through war, government intervention, erratic economic swings. Confined mostly to Japan, Finland, Germany, France and Italy, these have, in varying degrees, been buoyed by the cruise business boom that began in the early 1970s.

For the first four months of 1995, Disney Cruise Line held extensive discussions with all these shipyards. Each was invited to bid. "It was certainly one of the most difficult choices of my life," recalls Disney Cruise Line's President Art Rodney. "Negotiations continued right up to the deadline, and I wasn't ever certain until hours before who would get our nod."

On Tuesday, May 20, Rodney announced the decision. Cantieri Navali Italiani S.p.A., otherwise known by the acronym *Fincantieri*, was awarded the contract to build the yet-to-be-named Disney ship. "Naturally," adds Rodney, "We were thrilled. Fincantieri is a remarkable shipyard. It possesses the engineering skills, work force, financial clout, capacity and, best of all, imagination to undertake an assignment of this precision and magnitude for The Walt Disney Company."

Above left and right: THE *QUEEN MARY* AND THE *Q4* IN CLYDEBANK SHIPYARD, SCOTLAND.
Opposite: THE FINCANTIERI SHIPYARDS, ITALY, AT WORK ON THE *DISNEY MAGIC.*

"We invested a lot of resources in the preparation of the bid," recalls Enrico Buschi, Director, Cruise Ship Business, Fincantieri, in Trieste. "Yes, I must confess we were extremely interested in winning it. We believe we have a technical and commercial advantage that would be vital to this new client. And for us, a relationship with Disney is a matter of enormous prestige."

At that point, the detailed general arrangement plan was far from whole. Nearly a year and a half would pass before even the keel of the Disney ship could be laid. "The exterior ship design may have been complete," responds Buschi, "Yet, to me—you see, I'm foremost an engineer—the ship consisted of only meat and not the bones. To have a perfect body you need meat, bones, muscle. First, muscle."

Muscle translates into performance. The Disney Cruise Line team demanded a ship comfortable at 21 knots, supremely seaworthy, exceptionally secure in all conditions and—not to be overlooked—capable of transiting the Panama Canal. This was a tall order.

"We spent more than most," says Jon Rusten, "on hydrodynamics testing." These maneuvering and behavioral analyses were conducted on a scale model at a laboratory in Vienna. The process was painstaking. "Our Disney partners," remembers Buschi, "had set for us a target involving speed, power, shape, height and length. Our job was to carve the ship model to match these . . . points. . . . This is the first vessel, in my experience, that attains the absolute Panama Canal ship length maximum of 294 meters."

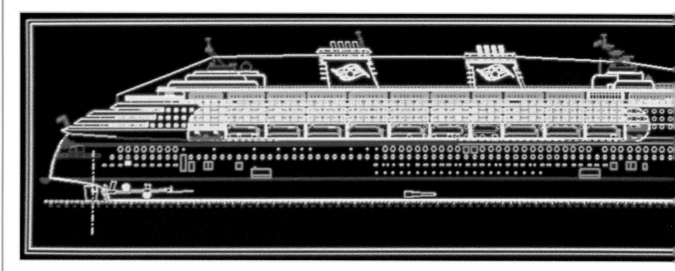

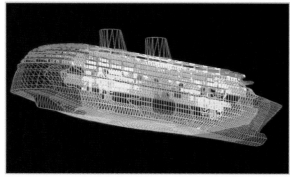

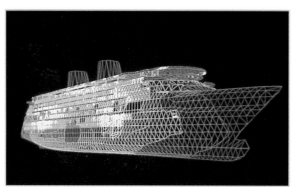

Rusten recalls the delight of Fincantieri's Vice Director, Project Management, GianFranco Bortaglia, when he was given the final test results: "He said he had never seen such a ship in all his career—and let's just say Mr. Bortaglia is no longer a young man. He said our design outperformed all others he had encountered in a lifetime, by an overwhelming margin."

Most alluring to the Fincantieri engineers was the ship profile. "I was so happy the Disney ship would not resemble a bus," states Enrico Buschi. "I work on this project every day and when I'm busy I probably don't stop to think how happy I am, but at the end of each day I can sense just how emotional this process has been . . . I say to friends that if they were not familiar with ships, they could close their eyes and they will begin to visualize a great ship with a dark hull and two wonderful funnels. . . . the Disney ship . . . It's the ship of the imagination."

While Fincantieri was moving forward with construction, a special team was coordinating the design

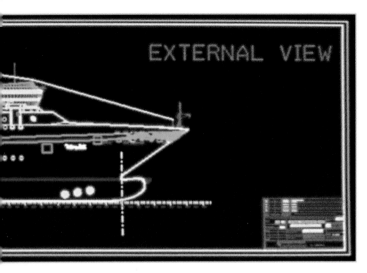

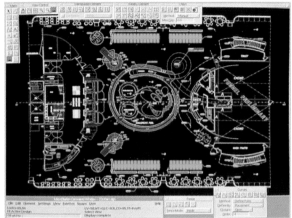

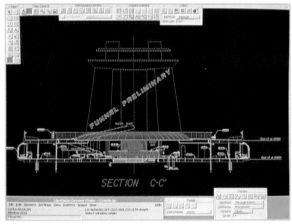

of the interior spaces of the *Disney Magic*. Once approved by the team, designs would make a stop in Scandinavia before reaching Italy. In Oslo, Yran and Storbraaten made sure all designs and materials conformed to exacting naval requirements. "We have had close to 20 people working day and night," reports Bjorn Storbraaten. "The drawings sent to Italy resemble a mountain. This is without doubt one of the most exciting projects in which I've ever participated . . . We put the music down on paper."

Every space onboard the Disney ship has been analyzed, every contemporary ship tradition held up to scrutiny. "One enormous breakthrough," recalls Al Weiss, President, Walt Disney World Resort, "was the dining experience." Traditionally, cruise ships offer a series of main dining rooms and a choice of seatings in each. Passengers must select their restaurant and their seating and then, more or less, hold to a habit. "But at Disney," asserts Weiss, "We reach for a more satisfying guest experience. It didn't seem to make

SHIP DESIGN

These pages: AUTOCAD™ DRAFTING DOCUMENTS OF THE SHIP WERE GENERATED BY THE TECHNICAL OFFICE AT FINCANTIERI SHIPYARD. THESE DOCUMENTS ALLOWED THE ARCHITECTS TO DESIGN AND ANALYZE THE STRUCTURE OF THE SHIP.

Opposite and above: THE ANIMATOR'S PALATE MOCK-UP ROOM
AND CONCEPT RENDERING BY THE ROCKWELL GROUP.

sense to confine our guests to one dining space. Art Rodney hit on a better idea."

Prior to joining Disney, Rodney had championed alternative shipboard dining. Now as President of Disney Cruise Line, he advanced the notion of combining an alternative restaurant with three rotating dining experiences. The principle was simple, according to Weiss. When a family visits a city for the first time, he notes, it normally tries a new restaurant each evening. Intuitively, it would appear, guests would prefer a similar experience at sea. Rodney and his colleagues demonstrated that if the Disney ship were to have three very different main restaurants, both guests and their waiter would be able to travel together, in each other's company from one dining experience to another: three different nights, three different restaurants, one waiter. Should they wish yet a fourth option, the stylish alternative restaurant, overlooking a high deck, awaits them.

Disney's paramount goal was to define this vessel, from the bones up, as family friendly. Paolo Simoniti, Project Coordinator, Fincantieri, was stunned by the Disney design. "Other ships have only one fifth the space dedicated to children as does Disney. The Disney way of treating kids so well, giving them so much room, will be . . . what can I say—revolutionary."

The Disney Cruise Line team saw the ship structured as a large community. At every stage of design, its creators would pause to consider the age group a particular space would attract, the amount of time to be spent there, the flow in and out of the area. When do families wish to be together, when apart? And how can you guarantee those wishes?

In an effort to create a seamless environment, the Disney team focused on every last detail. "In our hotels and at our attractions we consider the flow-through before we ever start building," says Al Weiss. "Naturally, we insisted on similar preparation for our

THE TEAM DEDICATED ITSELF TO ENSURING THAT SPACES AND ACTIVITIES
EXISTED FOR GUESTS OF ALL AGES. THIS DIORAMA MOCK-UP OF PIRATE'S
PLAYGROUND WAS GENERATED BY WALT DISNEY IMAGINEERS.

ship. Every space was worked and reworked—to get them perfect. Design documentation ensures we can deliver a guest experience that is functional."

"We were very impressed with Disney's knowledge of families on holidays and families in hotels," says Robert Tillberg of Tillberg Design AB of Sweden, which has coordinated the design of every stateroom and suite onboard ship. "Absolutely everything has been considered, from rounded corners to privacy to every square centimeter of storage space. The inspiration comes from the look of a very well-appointed luxury yacht matched to the cabin of a famous ocean liner. There is nothing like these cabins in the cruise industry today."

"We are excessive," observes Michael Eisner. "I must have attended 5 meetings about every room on the ship. I went to see life-size mock-ups of the ship's staterooms in Italy before we committed to any design detail. We change everything 3 or 4 times at least."

"Creativity is an open process," concludes Judson Green, President of Walt Disney Attractions. "The technique that led to the perfection of the ship design is typical of Disney. I always say I'll never accept the first 'take' on anything—no matter how brilliant. At Disney we have no shortage of ideas. Just turn on the spigots. We let ideas nurture. In the end, they always turn out better . . ."

By October 1996, every substantial detail of the ship had been finalized. In Norway and Sweden, mountains of architectural plans inspired by a legion of

THE WINDOW DESIGN IN PARROT CAY REFLECTS THE FUN, CASUAL DECOR
OF THE RESTAURANT. RENDERED ELEVATION BY DESIGN CONTINUUM.

THE DESIGN OF LUMIÈRE'S RESTAURANT IS ONE OF ELEGANT SIMPLICITY.
RENDERED ELEVATION BY DESIGN CONTINUUM.

THE LUSH, SUMPTUOUS DESIGN OF PALO, THE *DISNEY MAGIC*'S ADULTS-
ONLY RESTAURANT, OFFERS A UNIQUE DINING EXPERIENCE.

PALO

WARM WOODS,
VENETIAN GLASS,
CURVILINEAR WALLS,
AN EXHIBITION
KITCHEN AND STUDIED
LIGHTING ALL LEND A
TOUCH OF ELEGANCE TO
THE *DISNEY MAGIC*'S
ALTERNATIVE, ADULTS-
ONLY RESTAURANT.
PALO'S DESIGNER,
MARTIN DORFF, HOPES
THAT THE ATTENTION
TO DETAIL GIVEN TO
THIS RESTAURANT WILL
"ENGAGE EVERY ONE OF
THE SENSES."

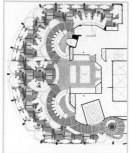

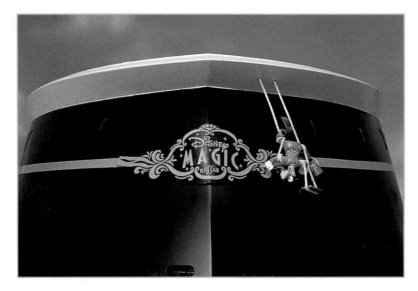

GOOFY LENDS A HAND IN MAKING *DISNEY MAGIC*
THE OFFICIAL NAME OF THE DISNEY CRUISE LINE'S FIRST SHIP.

designers were being transformed into general arrangement plans for delivery to Italy. Disney approval signatures were now accompanied by a number: "5989," the Fincantieri reference to the hull. Back in Orlando, the ship had advanced from number to name.

"There had been a contest," recollects Mike Reininger. "Everyone had been urged to submit suggestions. There were some good ones and a few doozies. . . . In the end, Michael [Eisner] insisted the ship celebrate Disney. If it wasn't going to be named after Walt Disney himself then it would be named after what he had created. Magic."

On October 21, 1996, the keel of the *Disney Magic* was laid. Like every other step of the design process, this procedure was not traditional to the cruise ship industry. Because of yard capacity and a tight schedule, Disney Cruise Line and Fincantieri resolved to initiate construction of the ship in two parts—the bow in the company's historic Ancona shipyard and the stern in its extensive facilities 100 miles to the north in Marghera, just outside Venice. Since modern ships are built essentially in "modules," one portion at a time added to the keel until the ship grows both laterally and vertically, it was a technical certainty the ship could be constructed in two locations, and once the bow was "ferried" by sea, it could, without hesitation, be matched to the aft.

While the technology for such a maneuver was never in doubt, the feat still raised eyebrows. Ultimately, the procedure would be the first of its kind in the cruise ship industry.

The challenge was to coordinate construction

Above and right:
DURING THE FLOAT
OUT, *DISNEY MAGIC*'S
BOW WAS TOWED OUT
OF ITS DRYDOCK AND
INTO THE ADRIATIC
SEA. GONDOLIERS
MET THE BOW AS IT
ENTERED THE SLOOP IN
VENICE LAGOON.

Above left to right: THE SHIP'S BOW, CONSTRUCTED IN ANCONA, AS IT PROGRESSED FROM SKELETAL STAGE TO FINAL EXTERIOR. PRIOR TO LEAVING ITS DRYDOCK, THE BOW WAS PLACED ON BALLAST TANKS, FLOATATION DEVICES TO AID ITS JOURNEY TO VENICE.

between both Fincantieri yards so that one hull would be ready for the other, simultaneously. By March, 1997, work on the bow section, comprising approximately one third of the vessel, was advancing slightly faster than that on the more extensive stern. Since tides, winds and production schedule limited the transfer maneuver to one week in April, additional shifts were added to the work in Marghera to ensure the stem's readiness. Finally, in early April, a date was set: Saturday the 12th. Mike Reininger was on hand in Ancona, as the bow's berth was flooded and final plates added to the makeshift stern. "All night long a storm raged and by dawn of the twelfth, my heart sank," recalls Reininger. "From my hotel room, I could hear the wind howling and I knew the seas were far too fierce for the bow to leave Ancona."

But the flooding of the berth continued all morning,

and at noon low clouds dispersed to reveal Ancona's imposing monastery, some 1000 years old, above the port. The winds abated and only a slow surge and roll seemed of concern for the two massive ocean-going tugs, just arrived from Trieste. "I knew by then we had it made," observed Mike Reininger.

With much celebration, the bow slowly edged out of its place of birth. Fishermen had readied their vessels to bring local children to view the sea-borne spectacle. Already the the bow's brilliant gold-painted ornamentation was in place. On it, a whimsical Mickey Mouse and his friends seemed, equally, to enjoy the nautical festivities. To the cries of *Topolino* (Mickey Mouse), the kids watched the outlandish procession of ocean-going tugs and one third elegant ship. By evening, the convoy was on the horizon.

For one day the bow of the *Disney Magic* traveled

BOW

THE BOW OF THE *DISNEY MAGIC* WAS BUILT AT THE FINCANTIERI SHIPYARD IN ANCONA. CARE HAD TO BE TAKEN WITH EVERYTHING FROM CRANING IN LARGE SECTIONS TO WELDING THESE SECTIONS TOGETHER, AND DOWN TO THE ELABORATE FILIGREE EMBLEM THAT DECORATES THE BOW.

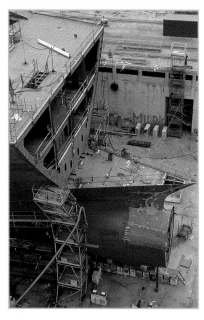

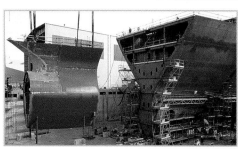

STERN

LOCATED 100 MILES FROM WHERE THE BOW WAS CONSTRUCTED, THE STERN WAS BUILT IN THE FINCANTIERI SHIPYARD IN MARGHERA. THE GLASS PORTHOLES HARKEN BACK TO MARITIME TRADITIONS OF THE *QUEEN MARY* AND *QUEEN ELIZABETH*. THE STREAMLINED STERN LINES CREATE AN ELEGANT YET CONTEMPORARY FINISH TO THE *DISNEY MAGIC*'S DESIGN. THE IMMENSE PROPELLER IS INSTALLED INTO THE SHAFTLINE PRIOR TO ITS BEING FITTED TO THE HULL.

Above left and right: THE SHIP'S IMPRESSIVE FUNNEL IS FLOATED IN AND CRANED INTO POSITION.
Opposite: THE MOMENT OF TRUTH, AS THE BOW AND STERN COME TOGETHER.

across the Adriatic, far from land. The 100-mile journey was completed by noon, Monday, April 14, when the flotilla reached Malamocca, entrance to the lagoons of Venice. Mike Reininger, Jon Rusten and other members of the Disney Cruise Line team were on hand to watch it proceed through a narrow channel leading to the industrial center of Marghera. Midway, three gondolas from nearby Venice met the procession. Onboard the gondolas were several accordionists. Thus, to the lilting cadence of "Santa Lucia," past arguably the world's most romantic city, the bow continued its journey until it reached the estuary outside Fincantieri's shipyards.

By now, the stern was ready: Its hold had been filled with fresh water, its berth flooded with sea water. This dual inundation allowed the stern to rest on a special cradle on the berth floor while the bow, now reversed and attached to yard winches, could be teased towards the stern, then matched, once the waters of the berth receded.

The fitting procedure took place over four days. A series of match points with interlocking plates would have to be joined. By eight on Monday evening, the two hulls were within 16 centimeters of each another. By next morning, the intervening distance had been reduced to 2; by Tuesday evening, joining of the two hulls could begin, with a variance of never more than one millimeter.

One notable difference between the *Disney Magic* and the ocean liners of long ago is their "skin." Until the late 1950s great ships were joined together by overlapping plates fastened one to the other by rivets. Such was the case with the *Queen Mary*, *Normandie* and many others. On close inspection, these ships presented an uneven surface, a mosaic of overlapping and underlapping steel.

Today, arc welding has been perfected and plates can be joined one to the other, edge to edge. The weld becomes integral to the steel; seams between plates are, in fact, stronger than the steel itself. When

Above: THE FLOAT TOGETHER OF THE BOW AND STERN.

a hull is complete—each plate welded to the other without any overlap at all—the result is not a collection of plates, but a solid, indivisible, "skin," its entire structure stronger than the sum of its parts.

By Friday, April 18, 1997, so it was with the *Disney Magic*: a seamless hull. But today was no occasion for pause; the pace of construction, in fact, accelerated. One of the ship's two graceful funnels, made in Trieste, was transported as deck cargo by tug to Marghera, then gently craned into position. One

month from the date the bow left Ancona, the ship's communication mast arrived also by tug and was hoisted into position above the *Disney Magic*'s bridge. This event was prelude to a fountainhead occasion.

On Monday, May 12, 1997, the *Disney Magic*'s berth, in Marghera, was flooded for the second time. The following morning at 10:30, the complete hull of the Disney ship floated for the first time. At noon, in sunlight filigreed by high clouds, a handful of Disney executives assembled on red carpets by the side of the

Above: THE SHIP'S BERTH IS FLOODED IN PREPARATION FOR THE FLOAT OUT.

ship they had nurtured to hear Corrado Antonini, Chairman and Chief Executive Officer of Fincantieri, and Art Rodney, President of Disney Cruise Line, summon the *Disney Magic* to a life on the sea. Hundreds of Fincantieri workers were on hand to celebrate the work of so many.

Rodney, accompanied by his wife Esta, looked up at the great blue black hull rising overhead and talked of this moment as "the dream of a lifetime." He thanked all those who had made this moment possible,

paused for a second, and interrupted his speech to pay special tribute to those workers far away in Ancona, whose dedication, like all others', would not go unrecognized.

Minutes later, to the blasts of horns, the flight of 50 doves, the salute of Mickey, Minnie, and Goofy and the cheers of many members of the press, the *Disney Magic* moved from her berth to a new home—beside a quay, in deep water.

Hereafter, the *Disney Magic* would be afloat.

❖ Life Onboard ❖

Walter Elias Disney and wife Lillian strolling along
the deck of the Italian luxury ship, the *Rex*, 1934.

INSIDE THE MODERN CLASSIC

5

Attention to detail and the fine art of storytelling have been applied most visibly for the interior spaces of the *Disney Magic*. From the staterooms to the stair landings, the dreammakers at Disney have infused their ship with specially commissioned artwork, murals, sculptures, intricate metal and woodwork, all of which combine to tell the story of a modern classic. "I see the interior as an emotional storyline," says Mike Reininger. "It must be approached not just as 'an interior,' but as a stage set. Our guests will walk onboard and then pass through spaces, from one story to another, all using a similar vocabulary that integrates them to the sea, legendary ocean liners and Disney. We intend the

story to have impact at every level. For that to occur we have adopted a central vision."

For over two years, distinguished artists and designers across North America and Europe as well as Disney Imagineers in Glendale have been working on commissions for the interior of the *Disney Magic*. A massive chandelier is coming to life in Seattle—the work of America's, if not the world's, most inventive glass artist. In New York, an innovative restaurant designer has dedicated his studio to one of the ship's four restaurants. His plan calls for at least five different expressions of wood—rich anigré, quartered ash, English sycamore, pear wood, ebonized oak—many of them last seen onboard the *Queen Mary*—to add a new sense of elegance to a very fresh interior.

Above, left and opposite: DETAILS FROM DEVELOPMENT ART FOR AN ELEVATOR MURAL BY STEVEN GUARNACCIA.

Original character sketches from the Disney archives, created by studio artists during the golden age of ocean liners, have been restored to be displayed onboard the *Disney Magic*. These sketches are unique yet intrinsically familiar. According to Nancy Rosen, art consultant to the Disney Cruise Line, "We may never have seen them individually before, but we recognize them."

Even lifeboats have not escaped Disney scrutiny. These, inspired by dependable Klinker- or lapstrake-styled fishing boats of long ago, will be reborn in Norway, using modern fiberglass to pay homage to maritime history but reconfigured as ultramodern life-saving tools.

The *Disney Magic* owes much to other legends.

Perhaps only a sleuth schooled in ocean-liner lore will be able to recognize every subtle reference. But futurists take note. Inspiration onboard the *Disney Magic* comes not merely from what liners once were, but the artistic limits they explored. The *Disney Magic* is the child of an age when ships were great because they were reflections of an era's best architects, artists, designers and artisans.

In the end, what makes this ship truly unique are the elements that only Disney storytellers can fashion. The ship's many details draw upon the rich history of Disney's art and stories. Every corner holds a new discovery for an explorer to stumble across. Even at journey's end, the ship still holds many surprises.

By all standards, old and new, the *Disney Magic* is a legend in the making.

Left: SILKSCREEN PRINT OF A PIRATE ADVENTURE MAP BY WALT DISNEY IMAGINEER JOHN HORNY, MADE FOR "PIRATES OF THE CARIBBEAN" IN DISNEYLAND PARIS.

Below: CABIN NUMBER SIGN DESIGNED BY DAVID CARTER DESIGN OF DALLAS, TEXAS.

Below left: SKETCH FOR "PIRATES OF THE CARIBBEAN" BY IMAGINEER MARC DAVIS, 1965.

Above and right:
STATEROOM MOCK-UPS.

Bottom: DISNEY'S ART
CONSULANT, NANCY
ROSEN, IDENTIFIED
THREE WONDERFULLY
APPROPRIATE DISNEY
MELODIES TO HANG
ABOVE STATEROOM
BEDS, INCLUDING THIS
SILKSCREEN REPRODUC-
TION OF *A DREAM IS A
WISH YOUR HEART
MAKES* FROM WALT
DISNEY'S *CINDERELLA*,
RELEASED IN 1948.

A Dream Is A Wish Your Heart Makes

A dream is a wish your heart makes——

Above: THE UNIQUE CHANDELIER THAT HANGS IN THE ATRIUM LOBBY WAS CREATED BY AMERICA'S PREMIER GLASS ARTIST DALE CHIHULY.

Above and right:
FANTASY SCULPTOR
JAMES GRASHOW OF
CONNECTICUT WAS
ASSIGNED TO INVENT
THIS IMAGINARY SHIP.

Opposite left:
RENDERING OF THE
ATRIUM LOBBY
DESIGNED BY HUGH
LATTA CONTINUUM,
ATLANTA, GEORGIA.
AT THE CENTER OF
THE LOBBY STANDS
A STATUE OF HELMS-
MAN MICKEY, CREATED
BY WALT DISNEY
IMAGINEERS.

ENTRY LOBBY

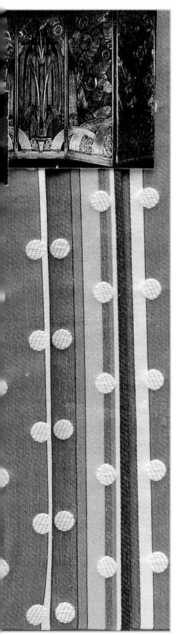

These pages: AMONG THE INTERIOR DESIGN INSPIRATIONS FOR THE ATRIUM LOBBY WERE FURNITURE, TABLES, LAMPS AND CARPET SAMPLES THAT EVOKED THE LUXURIOUS WORLD OF ART DECO.

ENTRY LOBBY

Above and right: THESE TWO 20-FOOT-LONG MURALS OF FANCIFUL MAPS WERE CREATED BY NEW JERSEY ARTIST STEVEN GUARNACCIA.

Opposite bottom right: THIS DETAIL OF THE MURAL AT RIGHT SHOWS TWO CHILDREN BUILDING A SAND CASTLE IN THE IMAGE OF CINDERELLA CASTLE, THE DEFINING SYMBOL OF THE MAGIC KINGDOM AT WALT DISNEY WORLD.

Bridge –*n.* An elevated, crosswise platform above the main deck from which the ship is navigated and controlled.

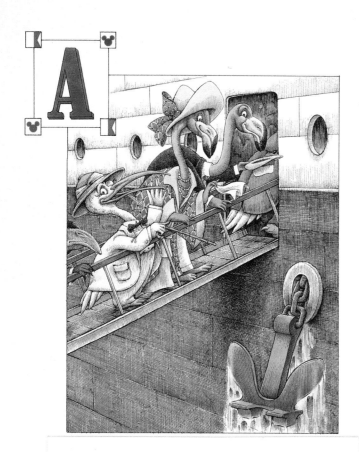

Anchors away –*interj.* The exclamation that a ship's anchor has been lifted in preparation to sail.

Captain –*n.* The officer in command of a ship.

NAUTICAL ALPHABET

TIM RAGLIN OF INDEPENDENCE, KANSAS, CREATED AN IMAGINATIVE, NAUTICAL-THEMED ALPHABET TO BE FEATURED ABOARD THE *DISNEY MAGIC*.

Deck chair –n. A folding chair with arms and a leg rest, found on the decks of a ship for use by passengers.

Even keel –n. The condition of a ship when it is level and floating evenly.

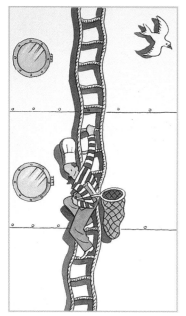

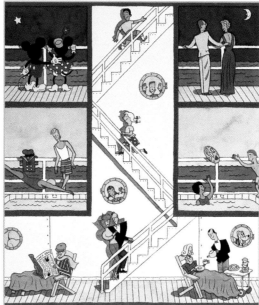

Above: ORIGINAL WATERCOLORS FOR THE FINAL ELEVATOR MURALS BY STEVEN GUARNACCIA. THE MURALS, TITLED "UP AND ABOUT," ARE SEEN THROUGH THE GLASS ELEVATOR DOORS FROM DECKS 6 TO 8 ON THE *DISNEY MAGIC.*

Right: DETAIL OF THE FINISHED MURAL.

Opposite: DETAIL FROM THE WATERCOLOR ART.

The ship can make 500,000 gallons of fresh water from sea water everyday while cruising.

8260 cups of coffee are served every day on board.

The 20,000 gallons of paint it takes to cover our ship could paint 2,000 average American homes.

SEAWORTHY FACTS

INSPIRED BY THE *BOOK OF COMPARISONS*, WHICH CELEBRATED THE MAIDEN VOYAGE OF THE *QUEEN MARY* IN 1936, STEVEN GUARNACCIA CREATED TEN ORIGINAL SILK-SCREENS ILLUSTRATING FUN FACTS ABOUT THE *DISNEY MAGIC*.

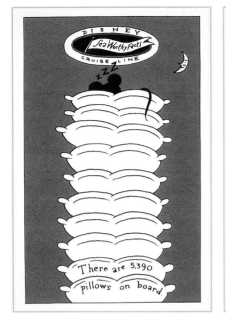

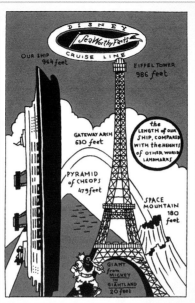

Walt Disney Theatre

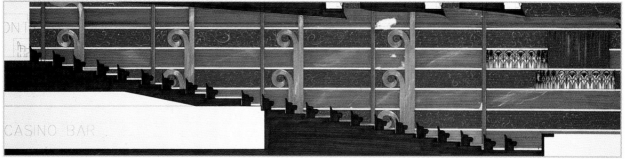

CASINO BAR

WALT DISNEY THEATRE

Above, middle left and opposite top: DESIGN INSPIRATIONS FOR THE WALT DISNEY THEATRE.

Above right: IMAGE OF WALT DISNEY USED FOR THE ENTRANCE MURAL.

Middle right, below and opposite bottom: CONCEPT RENDERINGS OF THE WALT DISNEY THEATRE.

OCEAN-RELATED STORY
SKETCHES, POSTERS AND
FILM STILLS FROM THE
WALT DISNEY ARCHIVES
DECORATE THE SHIP'S
STAIR LANDINGS.

Above: STILLS FROM
WALT DISNEY'S
HAWAIIAN HOLIDAY,
1937.

Left: FILM POSTER FROM
WALT DISNEY'S *KING
NEPTUNE*, 1932.

Above and right: FILM POSTERS FROM WALT DISNEY'S *MERBABIES*, 1938, AND *ALICE'S DAY AT SEA*, 1929.

Below: ONE OF TWO CIRCULAR PAINTINGS CREATED BY STEVEN GUARNACCIA AND INSPIRED BY ANCIENT GREEK VASE PAINTING. THE INFLUENCE OF CLASSICAL ART WAS PREVALENT IN THE ART DECO WORLD OF THE 1930S AS WELL AS ON LUXURY LINERS FROM THAT TIME.

Above: FILM STILL FROM *HOW TO BE A SAILOR,* 1949.

Top and opposite: STORY SKETCHES FROM *HOW TO BE A SAILOR,* 1949.

Above: RENDERING OF
THE *DISNEY MAGIC*'S
CARIBBEAN-THEMED
RESTAURANT, PARROT
CAY.

Left: HAND-PAINTED
STRAW HATS, CREATED
BY PENNY CARTER,
MARK THE ROUTE TO
PARROT CAY.

Right: INSPIRATIONS
FOR PROMENADE
LOUNGE.

Below: PROMENADE
LOUNGE RENDERING.

PROMENADE LOUNGE

Top: RENDERING OF
LUMIÈRE'S RESTAURANT.

Above: DESIGN INSPIRA-
TIONS FOR LUMIÈRE'S.

Left: LUMIÈRE'S GRAND
MURAL, FROM DISNEY'S
BEAUTY AND THE BEAST,
1991.

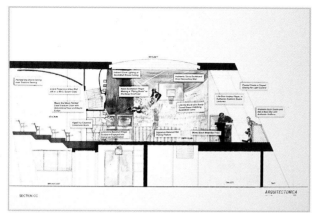

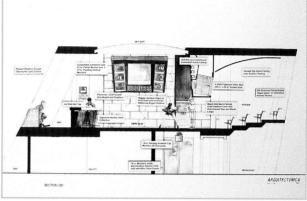

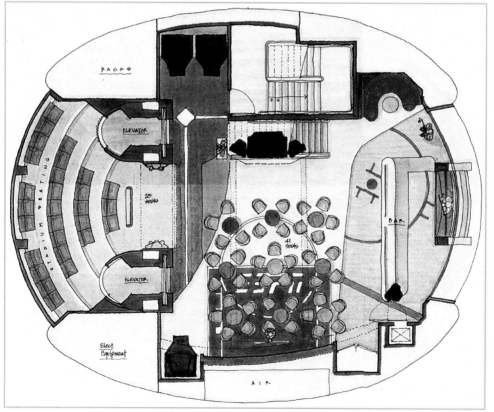

Above left and right:
RENDERED ELEVATION
CONCEPTS FOR THE
ESPN SKYBOX.

Left: ESPN FLOOR
PLAN.

Opposite top:
INSPIRATIONS FOR THE
FANTASY SOUND
STAGE, STUDIO SEA.

Opposite bottom right:
RENDERING OF STUDIO
SEA.

Opposite bottom left:
STUDIO SEA'S PORTAL
DESIGN.

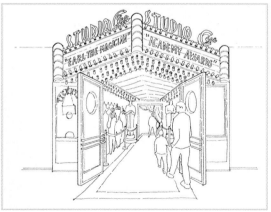

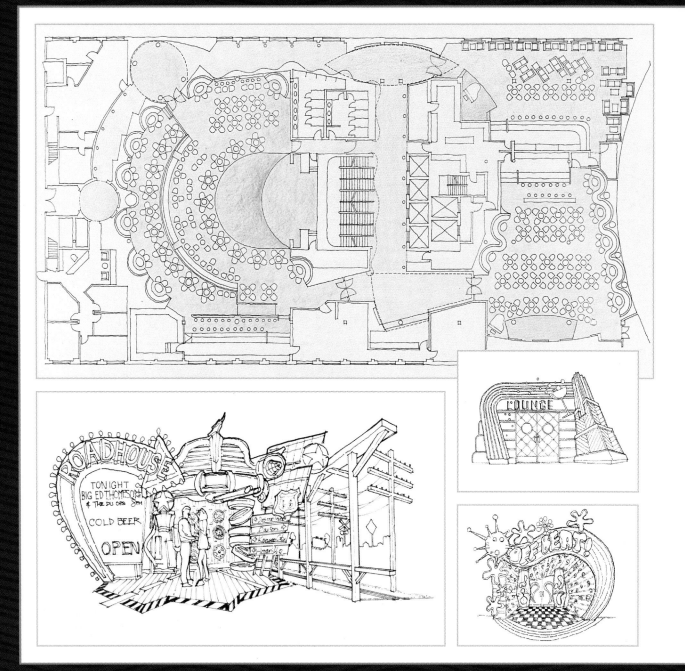

BOATS
INTERIORS
Seen Through
Hollywood
EYES

We're Rolling Speed

Above: INSPIRATION FOR
BEAT STREET.

Right top: OFF BEAT
COMEDY CLUB.

Below right: RENDERING
OF SESSIONS.

Opposite top: FLOOR PLAN
FOR BEAT STREET.

Opposite bottom: PORTAL
DESIGNS FOR THE CLUBS ON
BEAT STREET.

Above and left: PIRATES PLAYGROUND RENDERING AND DIORAMA.

Opposite page:
Top left: TILE MURAL CONCEPTS FOR DECKS 9 AND 10, ADAPTED FROM WALT DISNEY'S *HOW TO SWIM,* 1942.

Middle left: OCEANEER LAB RENDERING.

Top right: GOOFY POOL CONCEPT DESIGN.

Bottom right: MICKEY POOL CONCEPT DESIGN.

Bottom left: BUZZ LIGHTYEAR, FROM *TOY STORY,* 1995.

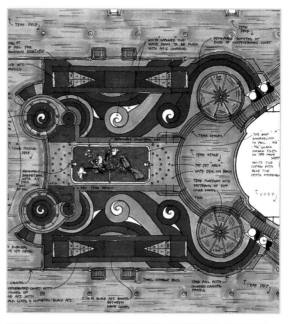

AFTERWORD

I n the interests of full disclosure, I must confess I've known about the *Disney Magic* for quite some time. In April 1994, thanks to a mutual friend at the Disney Institute, Mike Reininger met me in New York. During our discussions, Mike began to spellbind me with his vision of "the ship." The ship would be a "living legend," he affirmed, hands waving. It would "out-tradition tradition," it would strike everyone as the ultimate expression of both maritime history and the future.

Ever since I could look to the horizon, I have had more than a passing interest in the sea and great ocean-going vessels. As a child, I traveled with my family and three household pets onboard the S.S. *United States*, destination Le Havre. My mother had been insistent her impressionable kids not succumb to the allure of transatlantic airliners, the more efficient mode of travel, because, she affirmed, she wanted her brood to appreciate not how small the world is, but "its enormity." This early experience left me unable to resist a ship's whistle or the adventure of being outbound for remote ports.

Thus, in New York in 1994, when Mike Reininger described his dream of "the ship," he struck a nerve. Imagine helping create a vessel without equal anywhere in the world, a ship with an ancestry, not too foreign from the one on which I sailed.

Previous to my Disney interlude, I had always believed a camel to be a horse created by a committee. At Disney, I discovered otherwise. In this environment of collaborative creativity, where good ideas had to endure far beyond the honeymoon, there is a need for consensus. The object is not to realize notions that dazzle on impact, but to fashion concepts that are timeless, forever immune to the vicissitudes of fashion, weather, time and new management teams. After a while, I learned to trust this process. I watched everyone's "brilliant" notions reduced to essentials, made to conform to a greater Disney plan and then to evolve as threads in a tapestry. Today, most individual contributions to the *Disney Magic* are invisible.

Early in 1996 when I saw the final renderings of the vessel I was stunned. Here was a truly beautiful ship. The "retro" ship I had envisioned was now much better, more modern, Disney in every way. I gazed in awe, as impressed by the ship's elegance as by the collective creative achievement of the team that had designed it. Both inside and out, the ship is infused with a Disney tradition of attention to detail and creative whimsy that has long set the standard for extraordinary family entertainment.

Everything accompanying the birth of the *Disney Magic* has been an adventure. Here is a ship singular in every way. It defies convention and, in the end, it is the collective dream of many.